MW01133525

for

Knowing
God's Will

Other Women of Faith Bible Studies

Celebrating Friendship
Discovering Your Spiritual Gifts
Embracing Forgiveness
Experiencing God's Presence
Finding Joy
Growing in Prayer
Strengthening Your Faith

WOMEN OF FAITH™
BIBLE STUDY SERIES

Knowing
God's Will

Written by

EVELYN BENCE

General Editor

TRACI MULLINS

ZondervanPublishingHouse

Grand Rapids, Michigan

A Division of HarperCollins*Publishers*

Knowing God's Will
Copyright © 1998 by Women of Faith, Inc.

Requests for information should be addressed to:

📖 ZondervanPublishingHouse
Grand Rapids, Michigan 49530

ISBN: 0-310-21339-8

All Scripture quotations, unless otherwise indicated, are taken from the *Holy Bible: New International Version*®. NIV®. Copyright © 1973, 1978, 1984 by International Bible Society. Used by permission of Zondervan Publishing House. All rights reserved.

All rights reserved. No part of this publication may be reproduced, stored in a retrieval system, or transmitted in any form or by any means—electronic, mechanical, photocopy, recording, or any other—except for brief quotations in printed reviews, without the prior permission of the publisher.

General Editor, Traci Mullins
Cover and interior illustration by Jim Dryden
Interior design by Sue Vandenberg Koppenol

Printed in the United States of America

98 99 00 01 02 03 04 /❖ EP/ 10 9 8 7 6 5 4 3 2 1

CONTENTS

FOREWORD

The best advice I ever received was in 1955. I was twenty-three. Somebody had the good sense to say to me, "Luci, if you want to give yourself a gift, learn all you can about the Bible. Start going to a Bible class and don't stop until you have some knowledge under your belt. You won't be sorry." Having just graduated from college, I was living with my parents, and together we drove more than twenty miles to attend that class. We went four nights a week for two years. I've *never* been sorry.

Nothing I've ever done or learned has meant more to me than those classes. Unless I was on my deathbed, I didn't miss. I went faithfully, took notes, absorbed everything like a sponge, asked questions relentlessly, and loved *every* minute! (I probably drove the teacher crazy.)

Today, more than forty years later, this wonderful storehouse of truth is my standard for living, giving, loving, and learning. It is my Rock and Fortress, the pattern for enjoying abundant life on earth, and for all eternity. I know what I believe, and why. I'm open to change on my tastes, personal opinions, even some of my choices. But change my biblical convictions? No way! They're solid and secure, based on God's inerrant, enduring, and unchanging Word. There's nothing like learning God's truth. As he says, it sets you free.

Women of Faith Bible studies are designed to help you deal with everyday problems and issues concerning you. Experienced and wise women who, like the rest of us, want to know God intimately, have written these lessons. They encourage us to dig into the Scriptures, read them carefully, and respond to thought-provoking questions. We're invited to memorize certain verses as sources of support and guidance, to hide his Word in our heads and hearts.

The clever ideas in these studies make me smile. The stories move my spirit. There are valuable suggestions in dealing with others, quotations that cause me to stop and think. The purpose of every activity is to put "some knowledge under your belt" about the Bible and its relevance for life *this very day.*

Give yourself a gift. Grab your Bible, a pencil, notepad, cup of coffee . . . maybe even a friend . . . and get started. I assure you—you'll *never* be sorry.

LUCI SWINDOLL

HOW TO USE THIS GUIDE

Women of Faith Bible studies are designed to take you on a journey toward a more intimate relationship with Christ by bringing you together with your sisters in the faith. We all want to continue to grow in our Christian lives, to please God, to be a vital part of our families, churches, and communities. But too many of us have tried to grow alone. We haven't found enough places where we feel safe to share our heartaches and joys and hopes. We haven't known how to support and be supported by other women in ways that really make a difference. Perhaps we haven't had the tools.

The guide you are about to use will give you the tools you need to explore a fundamental aspect of your walk with God *with* other women who want to grow, too. You'll not only delve into Scripture and consider its relevance to your everyday life, but you'll also get to know other women's questions, struggles, and victories—many similar, some quite different from your own. This guide will give you permission to be yourself, to share honestly, to care for one another's wounds, and laugh together when you take yourselves too seriously.

Each of the six lessons in this guide is divided into six sections. Most you'll discuss as a group; others you'll cover on your own during the week between meetings.

A Moment for Quiet Reflection. The questions in this section are meant to be answered in a few minutes of privacy sometime before you join your group each week. You may already carve out a regular time of personal reflection in your days, so you've experienced the refreshment and insight these times bring to your soul. However, if words like "quiet," "reflection," and "refreshment" have become unfamiliar to you, let this guide get you started with the invaluable practice of setting aside personal time to think, to rest, to pray. Sometimes the answers you write down to the questions in this section will be discussed as a group when you come together; other times they'll just give you something to ponder deep within. Don't neglect this important reflection time each week, and include enough time to read the introduction to the lesson so you'll be familiar with its focus.

Knowing God's Heart. The questions in this section will take you into the Bible, where you and the women in your group can discover God's heart and mind on the subject at hand. You'll do the Bible study together, reading the Scriptures aloud and sharing your understanding of the passage so all of you can learn together what God has to say about your own heart and life, right now. While you don't need to complete the study questions prior to each group session, it will be helpful for you to read through this part of the lesson beforehand so you can begin thinking about your answers. There is a lot to cover in each lesson, so being somewhat familiar with the content before your meetings will save your group time when you actually do your study together.

Friendship Boosters. A big part of why you've come together is to deepen your friendships with other women and to support each other in meaningful ways. The questions and activities in this section are designed to link you together in bonds of friendship, faith, and joy. Whether you are meeting the other women in your group for the first time or are old friends, this section will boost the quality and pleasure in your relationships as well as give you opportunities to support each other in practical ways.

Just for Fun. God's plan for our lives certainly isn't all work and no play! Central to being a woman of faith is cultivating a joyful spirit, a balanced perspective, and an ability to enjoy life because of God's faithfulness and sovereignty. Every week you'll be given an idea or activity that will encourage you to enjoy your journey, laugh, and lighten your load as you travel the path toward wholehearted devotion together.

Praying Together. Nothing is more important than asking God to help you and your friends as you learn how to live out his truths in your lives. Each time you get together you'll want to spend some time talking to him about your individual and mutual concerns.

Making It Real in Your Own Life. You'll respond to these questions or activities on your own after group meetings, but don't consider them just an afterthought. This section is critical because it will help you discover more ways to apply what you've learned and discussed to your own life in the days and weeks ahead. This section will be a key to making God's liberating truths more real to you personally.

In each section, space is provided after each question for you to record your answers, as well as thoughts stimulated by others' answers during group discussion. While you can gain wisdom from completing parts of this guide on your own, you'll miss out on a lot of the power—and the fun!—of making it a group experience.

One woman should be designated as the group facilitator, but she needn't have any training in leading a Bible study or discussion group. The facilitator will just make sure the discussion stays on track, and there are specific notes to help her in the "Leader's Guide" section at the back of this book. Keeping your group size to between four and eight participants is ideal because then it will be possible for everyone to share each week. The length of time you'll need to complete the lessons together will depend largely on how much the participants talk, so the group facilitator will need to monitor the time to keep it under ninety minutes. The facilitator can also speed up or slow down the group time by choosing to skip some discussion questions or concentrate longer on others. If you decide to do this study in a larger group or Sunday school class, split up into smaller groups for discussion. Especially make sure no one gets left out of the process of building friendships and having fun!

Now that you've studied the map, your journey should go smoothly. Celebrate being women of faith as you travel together. *Enjoy!*

INTRODUCTION
Seek Ye First

When we get to heaven we can ask God why he didn't inspire an apostle to write a short epistle entitled "Ten Easy Steps to Knowing God's Will." A 1–2–3 list would untie some of the hard knots of life, wouldn't it? But God didn't dictate a how-to manual. Fortunately, neither is he silent regarding his will for us. He wove his loving guidance and perfect direction through scrolls written over centuries and preserved for his people through the generations.

Some of God's guidance is given by Jesus himself, who laid out a foundational principle: "Seek first [God's] kingdom" (Matt. 6:33). Yes, we are told to *seek*. And yet for many Christians the search becomes a burdensome responsibility. Maybe because we become preoccupied with seeking *our* place in the kingdom. Or maybe because the *search for* God's will—rather than actually *living in* God's will—becomes our life task, our constant burden.

If you know that heavy feeling, take heart. Note the words of Jesus, who also promised, "My burden is light" (Matt. 11:30). Read that sentence again. Listen to it with your heart. Set aside the weight of responsibility and begin this study with joyful anticipation. Seek God's kingdom. Listen with your spiritual ears, and receive God's word with gladness!

This is not an exhaustive study of Scriptures dealing with the topic of knowing or doing God's will. Nor is it the 1–2–3 how-to manual many of us long for. But here, as we look into a few passages, we can get a handle on God's ways and our ways as we step lightly into the good works he has prepared for us to do.

> *"Seek ye first the Kingdom of Heaven . . ."*
> *and the burden will be light!*
>
> EUGENIA PRICE

God's Goodwill

God's will. Sometimes it sounds ominous. If our hearts aren't ready to receive it or obey it, the prospect of asking to know it can be frightening. *What if he wants me to go to Antarctica or Zimbabwe? I hate the cold. I hate the heat. Never, no way. Not me!*

Our trust or distrust of God's goodwill toward us can be evident in the way we approach the topic of God's will. What do we really believe about his purposes and our role in his plans? Are we ready to place ourselves in his hands? Are we ready to position ourselves under the spout of blessing? Are we ready for any surprises he might have for us, confident that he is a God of perfect love?

Let's start our study by looking at the gospel account of a woman who was clearly ready to receive God's word and will: Mary, Jesus' mother. Many women put Mary on a lofty unreachable spiritual plane. Yes, in one sense she was unique in all history. But a closer look at Luke's gospel may reveal some surprises. You may have more in common with Mary than you think!

> *God is looking for people who are available as His instruments.*
>
> GIEN KARSSEN

A Moment
for Quiet Reflection

1. When you think of "God's will for me," name one fear that comes to mind.

Speaking in front of a large group of strangers.

2. Write a brief (one-sentence) prayer. Start the prayer, "Lord, I am ready for you to show me ..." Finish the sentence by identifying what you would like to know or learn from him during the course of this six-lesson study.

... the direction you would have me go in my life to serve you.

3. Copy your prayer. Tape one copy to the inside front cover of this booklet. Put your name on the second copy and take it with you to the first group gathering.

Knowing God's Heart

1. The gospel of Luke gives insight into Mary's character and our own standing as women in Christ. Read Luke 11:27–28. What is easier for you—"hearing" from God or obeying him? Discuss your answers.

2. Read Luke 1:26–40, 45. Then have the group close their eyes as one person rereads aloud the greetings from God's messenger (verses 28 and 30). Reread it yet again, trying to receive the blessing as "your own." Does it unsettle you, as it did Mary? If you feel the need to answer "but . . ." in response to the blessing, discuss the "what" and "why" of the "but."

3. It seems the messenger or the message made Mary afraid. Does being "favored by God" make you afraid of anything? What and why?

4. Consider the angel's greeting *and* closing (verses 28 and 37) as if they were a frame around his message. Describe the qualities of that frame.

5. If you can see God's will for you as being similarly framed, do your feelings change their shape, size, or position? Explain.

6. What specific information about the future (the next thirty years) did the angel give Mary?

7. When thinking about God's will for you, do you itch for "details" so you can feel more on top of what might happen? Think of a specific situation in which you would like to know God's will. What "details" do you wish God would reveal to you?

8. What did Mary's responses (verses 34 and 38) say about her readiness to hear and do God's will?

9. As a group, reword Mary's parting response to the angel (verse 38) in several ways. In one version include the phrase "God's will." If one version more than others strikes you as "your" heart-prayer, explain why.

10. The rest of Mary's life would be full of surprises. One of those surprises came when Mary went to visit Jesus, now grown and preaching in a nearby town. Read Luke 8:19–21. If you had been Mary, how would this have made you feel? As a Christian believer, how does it make you feel?

Mary   Myself

11. These verses in Luke 8 draw us back to the blessing of "hearing and obeying God's word" found in Luke 11:28 (question 1). Read again Luke 11:28. To encourage each other, tell of one grace or blessing you've experienced in the past as you heard and obeyed God's good will.

12. Read Luke 2:19, in which Luke describes Mary's reaction to curious life events. Share a personal experience, where you've been able to make sense of God's way only after you've had time for quiet reflection. How has this reflection helped allay your fears of God's will for you?

Lord ... May I relish the joy of knowing
you are full of wonderful surprises.
LUCI SWINDOLL

Friendship Boosters

1. To get better acquainted with one another and your individual goals for this study, read aloud to the group your prayers written before the session. Throughout the study the other women in your group might provide valuable insight as they remember your prayer.

Place all your prayers in a bowl or basket and then pick out one prayer-slip other than your own. Tape the request inside the back cover of this booklet. Throughout the next six weeks stay particularly attuned to the woman who wrote this prayer and pray along with her about her request. Send her an occasional encouraging note, or call to ask how God is revealing his will to her.

2. Mary's attitude and behavior in response to God's will still inspire us today. As a group allow yourselves to "think big." Imagine your families, neighborhoods, or the world fifty years from now. What blessings do you hope will remain as a result of *your* ready response to God's word? Sprinkle a little humor into your conversation and see where it takes you. Who knows how God might spark up possibilities for what you see as a far-fetched impossibility.

Just for Fun

After receiving the angel's message, Mary may have lived with some apprehension. But she also surely sensed that something wonderful was about to happen. Using folded white or colored typing paper and colored markers, make a greeting card to send or hand to someone else in the group. The message should relay good wishes and prayers for the expected coming of "something wonderful," as you all become increasingly ready to receive God's good will.

Praying Together

Be open and honest before God, bringing to him your questions and feelings about knowing and walking in his will. If many in your group are "afraid of surprises," consider the Luci Swindoll prayer above, asking God to help you learn to delight in his good will, whatever surprises it may bring. End the prayer by expressing your confidence in God, that "he who began a good work in you will carry it on to completion until the day of Christ Jesus" (Phil. 1:6).

> *What He teaches you to see He also teaches you to do.*
> ANDREW MURRAY

Making It Real
in Your Own Life

1. Before getting out of bed every morning this week, sing the first lines of "Joy to the World" by Isaac Watts, making one significant word change: "Joy to the world, the Lord is come! Let [your name] receive her King; Let every heart prepare him room. And heav'n and nature sing!" Then consider what you can do that day to ready your heart to make room for Christ and his will for you. (Note that "Joy to the World" was not written as a Christmas song; it is loosely based on the praises of Psalm 98.)

2. Identify one area of your life in which you want to know God's will. Set your mind on *expectation* of what God wants to birth through you and your heart as you learn to say *Let it be* according to your will and word.

3. If any fear of God's will still niggles, repeat the honest prayer of a father asking Jesus to heal his child: "I do believe; help me overcome my unbelief!" (Mark 9:24).

> *Trust in the LORD with all your heart and lean not on your own understanding; in all your ways acknowledge him, and he will make your paths straight.*
>
> PROVERBS 3:5–6

Beyond Intuition

You may feel assured that God's will is good, and even that your heart is ready to receive his will. But then another question may arise: Is knowing or discerning God's will anything more than having a good intuitive sense? After all, our "women's intuition" can broadcast some pretty loud messages at times!

Few people deny that many women are just naturally adept at discerning when something feels right and when "something feels wrong here." Margaret Mead suggests that women's intuition is a result of our "age-long training in human relations."

But the most highly honed natural instincts . . . the accumulated training of generations . . . the longest self-help course—all fall short of the vast wisdom and knowledge available to God's children.

In this lesson we'll look at passages from several letters written by the apostle Paul to believers in various cities. Woven throughout these letters we can identify some resources available to Christians who are eager to know—and do—God's will.

> *And this is my prayer: that your love may abound more and more in knowledge and depth of insight, so that you may be able to discern what is best.*
> PHILIPPIANS 1:9–10

A Moment
for Quiet Reflection

1. Think about your understanding or experience of "women's intuition." How is it different from your understanding or experience of discerning God's will?

2. In your mind return to the days of childhood. Remember playing a version of hide-and-seek, where one person hides a small object, such as a thimble? As I remember the game, the "seeker" hunts, the "hider" gives clues. "Getting warmer ... colder," until the object is found. Do you think God plays "warmer-colder" games with his children seeking his will? Give reasons for your answer and discuss them later (as noted) with the group.

Knowing God's Heart

1. First Corinthians 2:16 says that we as believers "have the mind of Christ." What does this mean to you and for you?

2. Let's look at the larger context of this "mind of Christ" verse; read 1 Corinthians 2:4–16. Work together to summarize what resources are available to those who have "the mind of Christ" in them. (Look especially at "not A, but B" statements.)

3. Read Romans 12:1–2. Discuss or "walk through" the process Paul describes. What leads to what?

4. Brainstorm together specific things any of you might do this week to "renew your mind" or renew the "mind of Christ" within you.

5. In another letter Paul greets fellow Christians in Colosse. Read Colossians 1:6–9. He prays for them to be filled with the knowledge of God's will. Discuss possible reasons why someone might want to know God's will.

6. Continue reading in Colossians 1:10–14. What reasons for knowing God's will are on his list? Which of your identified reasons (question 5) jibe with Paul's "in order that"?

7. Discuss times when you think you didn't discern God's will, because you wanted "knowledge" for the wrong reasons.

8. In verses 9–14 Paul's prayer outlines a process that begins and ends with God and virtually drips with blessing—resources available to God's children. In light of this list, discuss your personal reflections about whether God plays holy hide-and-seek.

9. Next time you feel as if God is playing hide-and-seek, what one or two resources noted in this lesson will you claim as your own? Discuss the "why" behind your personal choices.

10. Reread Colossians 1:12. Paul's letters to Corinth, Rome, and Colosse are addressed to "the saints" or those "called to be saints" or the "holy and faithful." Paul obviously saw the potential of the friends and acquaintances—the ordinary Christians—in his network. Let's say Paul were writing a letter to your study group. "To the saints gathered in [your town] . . ." What might be his one-sentence (or maybe one-word!) summary of the Scriptures studied in this lesson?

> *God is great, and therefore He will be sought; He is good, and therefore He will be found.*
>
> AUTHOR UNKNOWN

Friendship Boosters

1. Ephesians 5:17 reads: "Do not be foolish, but understand what the Lord's will is." After saying we should be "filled with the Spirit" (verse 18), Paul offers his own friendship booster, saying, "Speak to one another with psalms, hymns and spiritual songs" (verse 19).

As a group make up a spiritual song of encouragement. Don't worry about talent. Be creative. One person can start, making up words and tune for one line, each person adding a new line of her own, all the way around the room. (Or agree on a recognized tune and have each person make up one line of new words.)

The spontaneous tune may get "lost in the wind." But write down the words—as if they were the letter you corporately write to your own circle of Christian brothers and sisters (as Paul wrote letters to his).

2. In both Greek and Hebrew the word *spirit* is the same as the word for *wind*. In physical terms think about your being "in the wind" and the wind being "in you" as you breathe. At the end of this session or during the week go out and take a brisk walk with one or more friends. Take conscious note of your breath, and discuss any new insights you're learning about your life in and with God's Spirit.

Just for Fun

Let the child in you come out and play—not a raucous yard game but a quiet game of hide-and-seek. Send one person out of the room. The rest of the group can hide a small object. Then while the "seeker" hunts, the group gives warmer-colder clues until the object is found. To make the game more interesting, the group should not speak words—only make "warm" or "cold" noises (whatever you perceive "warm" or "cold" to sound like). Or maybe give silent clues, as in charades. Go for silly! Let yourselves have a laugh.

Praying Together

Return to Paul's prayer for the Colossian Christians. Praying together for each other, touch on the points or phrases of Paul's prayer. End with a prayer like that of Epaphras, whom Paul cites again at the end of Colossians: "He [Epaphras] is always wrestling in prayer for you, that you may stand firm in all the will of God, mature and fully assured" (Col. 4:12).

> *We are not to depend on our unenlightened human understanding but upon our human judgment and common sense enlightened by the Spirit of God.*
> HANNAH WHITALL SMITH

Making It Real in Your Own Life

1. In the "Making It Real" section of Lesson 1, you identified one area of your life in which you want to know God's will—*expectation*. This week set your mind on *transformation* and *renewal*. As you look at your area of concern, ask the Holy Spirit to quicken your mind in terms of available options. Maybe you see only two "roads" open to you, but in a larger view, there may be ten viable options for action. Try thinking "outside the box" this week. Gather a bit of information. Network. Write down every good (even not-so-good) suggestion. (In later lessons we'll explore ways to "sift" the options.)

2. The book of Proverbs is a treasure chest of wisdom that gives practical pointers for discerning the "right" from the "wrong" course of action. And Proverbs is conveniently laid out in thirty-one chapters. Commit to reading one chapter a day for the next month. Highlight or copy into a journal proverbs that speak to your current concerns.

> *For this God is our God for ever and ever;*
> *he will be our guide even to the end.*
>
> PSALM 48:14

Asking for Guidance

Many Christians believe that God has promised special resources to his children. Yet they fail to take advantage of them. A few years ago Mary, a single mother, was unemployed, running out of money, and beginning to panic. Her four-year-old son sensed his mother's anxiety and gave her some prayer advice that stopped her cold. "Mom, you've just got to pray: God help me, help me, help me ... until he does." That nudge reminds Mary, even now, to turn her eyes on her Lord instead of obsessing over the problems at hand.

In this lesson we will turn to three scriptural passages that offer insight into our quest for divine guidance. The Luke version of what we know as "the Lord's Prayer" (or "the Our Father") is given by Jesus in response to a disciple's question: "Lord, teach us to pray" (Luke 11:1). The longer Matthew version doesn't come with that introduction, but let's look at it with that "Lord, teach us" request at heart. And then we'll go on to two prayers in the New Testament Epistles.

Ready? Let's explore the Word and discuss what we discover about principles for requesting God's guidance and discovering his will for our lives.

> *If you feel stuck, bring your whole self to Christ, not just the problem, but you. Ask God to change your heart. Commit yourself to pray to that end. It's God's heart to give good gifts to his children.*
>
> SHEILA WALSH

A Moment
for Quiet Reflection

1. Surely the Lord's Prayer is the best-known, most memorized Christian prayer in the world. If you know it by heart, say it aloud as you might in church. Then say it silently—pausing after each phrase to let your prayer echo through your spirit. As you speak to God, what does God speak to you? (If you don't know the prayer, read it in Matthew 6:9–13.)

2. As you walk toward the place where your Bible study will be held, whisper the prayer a third time, preparing your heart for the study.

Knowing God's Heart

1. Read Matthew 6:7–8, which introduces the Lord's Prayer. Contrast this with Paul's succinct instruction to "Pray without ceasing" (1 Thess. 5:17 KJV). Are these two instructions—don't babble but pray without ceasing—contradictory? Why or why not?

2. Tell the group of a time when you were certain that God heard a short, to-the-point prayer for guidance.

3. Jesus' model prayer provides a frame within which we can boldly present to God any specific request for guidance. Read Matthew 6:8–13. Consider this quote by Terry Fullam *(Living the Lord's Prayer)*: "To ask that 'Thy will be done' is to ask that 'Thy kingdom come.' It is to ask that God's rule be established in the hearts, the wills, of men, women and children everywhere." Tell of a time when you had to struggle to get from "my will be done" to "thy will be done." (You might think especially in terms of "letting go" of your desire to "rule" a spouse or child.)

4. What does the Lord's Prayer ask God to do for you? To answer this question, as a group paraphrase the prayer as a series of personal "prayer requests."

5. Read Romans 1:10–17. This refers to a heart-prayer of Paul regarding God's direction and will for him. What does Paul pray for and why?

6. Christians often talk about praying for "open doors." Once a door is "unlocked" for us, what do we need to do?

7. Tell the group about a time when it was difficult for you to "step through" an unlocked—or open—door. Why was the step hard to take?

8. Sometimes knowing God's will is a matter of knowing which of many "open doors" we should walk through. Read James 1:5–6. What are *we* to do—when and why? What does God do—when and how?

We Do   God Does

9. Discuss a time when you prayed for God's guidance and still felt emotionally churned up like the waves of the sea. What do you think contributed more to your turbulence— lack of wisdom or lack of faith?

10. Discuss one area of your life—this week—in which you "lack wisdom." With help from the group, state a one-sentence prayer that lays your request before God.

> *Prayer reduced to a recipe will not work.*
> *Prayer is not the key that unlocks the doors of heaven*
> *or moves the hand of God; Christ is!... Our prayers*
> *may indicate what we want but any realized desires*
> *are bestowed on us by the gracious hand of Christ.*
> *The more we ask in accordance to His will, the more*
> *He will grant to us in response to our petitions. This is*
> *why it is important that our wills, wants and wishes go to*
> *the cross before our petitions go to the throne.*
>
> JUDSON CORNWALL

Friendship Boosters

1. Turn to the prayers written by you and other group members in Lesson 1—the ones you taped inside the front and back covers of your study book. At this midpoint of the study, read the prayers aloud again. Discuss insights gained in regard to one another's questions. Note questions still unanswered and agree to help one another pray and work toward finding answers.

2. Note again Romans 1:11–12, where Paul longs to be "mutually encouraged" by the faith of others. Mutually encourage the group by telling one another of a time when a faith-full prayer for guidance was answered.

Just for Fun

With appreciation and respect for the innocence of youth, relate any memories you have of childhood prayers—your own or those of friends or family—that now seem humorous. Enjoy a good laugh. (If childhood prayer requests don't come to mind, think of children's requests to adults.) Might some of our adult prayers seem similarly humorous to God? As a preacher recently quipped, "If you want to make God laugh, tell him your plans."

Praying Together

On behalf of each other, ask God to open your hearts to his will and his guidance. Your group may or may not know the hymn-prayer "Spirit of God, Descend Upon My Heart." If you know the tune, you might *sing* the following verse. Or just say the prayer, written by George Croly:

> *I ask no dream, no prophet ecstasies,*
> *No sudden rending of the veil of clay,*
> *No angel visitant, no opening skies;*
> *But take the dimness of my soul away.*

> *The thought of him to whom that prayer goes*
> *will purify and correct the desire.*
>
> GEORGE MACDONALD

Making It Real
in Your Own Life

1. Turn your attention again to the area of your life in which you're seeking God's will. Write a prayer that includes a specific request for guidance in sorting through your available options. Begin a journal page with the heading "Questions for God." Over the next several weeks add questions that arise about your question or impending decision.

2. Begin another page on which you can list pros and cons for various options. Over the next weeks note positives and negatives as they come to mind. Put a date next to your entries so you can track any mood swings or movements of the Spirit in your life.

> *Now to him who is able to do immeasurably more than all we ask or imagine, according to his power that is at work within us, to him be glory....! Amen.*
> EPHESIANS 3:20–21

Who's Calling?

The Reverend Peter Daly used a telephone metaphor to describe God's call: "You can't stop that insistent ringing until you answer the phone" (*Washington Post*, June 18, 1989).

And yet for most of us on most days, "hearing" God's direction is usually not as evident as hearing the telephone ring. Or if it is, the "caller ID" is not glowing in digital letters.

A hundred years ago Hannah Whitall Smith published some keen insights about discerning God's will. In *The Christian's Secret of a Happy Life*, she wrote, "We must never forget that 'impressions' can come from other sources as well as from the Holy Spirit." She advises that we test impressions, which might be influenced by persuasive personalities around us, our physical infirmities, and even our "spiritual enemies."

She also gives positive direction: "If you have an impression of duty, you must see whether it is in accordance with Scripture, whether it commends itself to your own higher judgment and also whether the way opens for its carrying out. If any one of these tests fails, it is not safe to proceed, but you must wait in quiet trust until the Lord shows you the point of harmony."

Let's dig into a few scriptural passages that show how God directs and how we can become discerning listeners.

> *No special guidance will ever be given about a point on which the Scriptures are explicit, nor could any guidance ever be contrary to the Scriptures.*
>
> HANNAH WHITALL SMITH

A Moment
for Quiet Reflection

1. Think of a time when you quickly ran away from a situation out of fear—rather than waiting to walk in faith and God's strength.

2. Think back over the last two weeks. From where have many of your "impressions" come? What do you currently do to "test" whether or not they are of God?

Knowing God's Heart

1. Read 1 Thessalonians 5:12–24. As you read, look for elements of God's will for all Christians. Which is hardest for you to live out? (To illustrate, give an example of a particular day/encounter in your life.)

2. Do you think that walking in the will of "the God of peace" (verse 23) means that we will feel *no* fear? Why or why not?

3. Read 2 Timothy 3:14–16. This may be a well-worn passage to you. Look at it with fresh eyes and in terms of "testing" God's will. Discuss a time when you turned to the Scriptures in search of guidance for a particular decision. How did the Scriptures "equip" you for God's work?

4. Think of a course of action you're considering. Read the following brief Scripture passages. For each, name a guideline for acting in God's will. Tell the group a few details of your upcoming decision and together put your intended action through the "grid" of Scripture. Discuss what this "test" shows you about the "rightness" or "wrongness" of what you're thinking of doing.

    a. Proverbs 11:3

    b. Proverbs 13:10

    c. 2 Timothy 1:7

    d. 1 Corinthians 16:8–9

    e. 1 Corinthians 10:31

    f. Acts 17:11

5. Read Isaiah 30:15–18. Consider the structure: A . . . but B . . . yet C. What characteristics are shown of us humans and of God?

6. Tell the group about a time when you ran away from a situation out of fear—rather than waiting to walk in faith and God's strength. (See "Quiet Reflection" question 1.)

7. Next time you are feeling ready to overreact out of fear— rather than waiting to act in faith and God's strength, what faith-full steps can you take? (Discuss how you might live out the truth of Isaiah 30:15.)

8. First Thessalonians 5:14 (question 1) warned against "being idle." Isaiah 30 suggests we should not get ahead of God. What might "active waiting" for God mean as you try to discern God's direction for you? Share specific examples from your own lives.

9. Now read Isaiah 30:19–22. Discuss times in your life when you've felt confirmation of God's direction "whispered" from "behind you" after you took an initial step of faith—in quietness and trust.

10. If you continued to obey the direction of that voice, what were some of the results?

> *We need to ask ourselves why we "feel" a particular course to be right, and make ourselves give reasons—and we shall be wise to lay the case before someone else whose judgment we trust, to give his verdict on our reasons.*
>
> J. I. PACKER

Friendship Boosters

1. Help each other grasp the wonderful truth found in Isaiah 30:18: "The LORD longs to be gracious to you." Before you leave this study or during the week, make one "gracious" gesture toward every woman in your study group. Do this in any way you wish.

2. Consciously be aware of how you receive the gracious gestures of fellow women of faith. Receive grace with grace! Challenge and encourage each other to be gracious receivers.

Just for Fun

Listen this week to your very favorite piece of music. Through music let God speak grace to your spirit. Play it for a friend or family member and tell that person why you like it so much—because it's beautifully crafted? Because it reminds you of a special person or event? Because it's lively or serene? . . .

Praying Together

In your prayer time together, allow some silence. Anyone should pray aloud as she feels led by the Spirit, but do not feel compelled to jump in and talk just to fill the silence. Listen as God's Spirit whispers to yours—through the voice of others in the group or heart to heart. After your prayer time, tell the group of any word received to your heart, if appropriate.

> *God never said that He would lay out His plan for your life in cinemascope so you can view it in its entirety. What He does promise is to lead you as you go; to direct you day by day; to show you His will hour by hour.*
> TONY CAMPOLO

Making It Real
in Your Own Life

1. Consider again your current area of concern. Continue to list positives and negatives for various options and eliminate any clear noncontenders. Start a new journal page titled "Steps to Action." If you were to test to see whether doors were "open" or "locked," what would be your next action steps for your options?

2. Refer to the journal in which you've been recording the proverbs that speak to your current concerns. What specific direction do these proverbs give you so far?

> *Breathe through the heats of our desire*
> *Thy coolness and thy balm;*
> *Let sense be dumb, let flesh retire;*
> *Speak through the earthquake, wind, and fire,*
> *O still, small Voice of calm!*
>
> JOHN GREENLEAF WHITTIER

It's Not Magic

We may wish for a secure life, where we'd always know exactly what we're walking into. *Just tell me what to do, and I'll do it. Just tell me that I'm not about to make a mistake I'll live to regret.* Wouldn't it be nice if we could live by sight and not by faith?

But think again about the story of Mary, Jesus' mother, and how very little information the angel gave to her. And Paul, who asks his readers to understand and know God's will, makes it clear that "The righteous will live by faith" (Rom. 1:17).

Chapter 16 of Acts provides a case study of how Paul himself seems to have discerned what his next step should be. Throughout much of this chapter, the writer of Acts, Luke, uses the pronoun *we*, indicating that he was traveling with Paul and was therefore a firsthand witness to decisions and how they were made.

Let's look at Acts 16:6–40, taking it a paragraph or so at a time. From Paul's experiences, we can home in on various "decision points" to see what we can learn about discerning and doing God's will.

> *God does not always work according to a set pattern.*
> GIEN KARSSEN

A Moment
for Quiet Reflection

1. Think back over your relationship with God. In a quick review, jot down three or four different ways God has used to show you what direction to take.

2. Think of a time when God used a particular person as a "guidepost," helping you clarify issues as you made a decision. Write that person a quick note of thanks. Such people may never realize the role they have played in your life as encourager or wisdom giver. If you've lost track of this special person, say a prayer of thanks and blessing.

Knowing God's Heart

1. Read Acts 16:6–8. Identify Paul's "decision points." How and why did he make his decisions?

2. Share with the group any experience you've had of "being kept" from proceeding with plans. How did you know something "wasn't right"?

3. Read Acts 16:9–12. A vision! Maybe you've hoped for one. It seems the vision required interpretation. Did Paul's companions agree or disagree with his "conclusion"? What insight might this passage give about basing major decisions on directives that someone else "heard from God"?

4. Read Acts 16:13–15. Why did they go to the river? What (who) convinced them to stay at Lydia's house?

5. Tell of a decision you have made in the last two days in which a choice—which you feel was in God's will—was guided by seemingly nonspiritual signposts.

6. Read Acts 16:16–19. As directly quoted, the girl is speaking truth, so why might Paul have been "troubled"? (Consider several reasons.)

7. How does this scene help you as you try to "test the spirits" and react to the troublesome negatives in your life?

8. Now read verses 25–28 of Acts 16. Paul could sing and praise God in prison. Tell of a time when God's grace sustained you through pain and trauma—even to the point of giving you a song in your heart.

9. Alice in Wonderland might say this story gets "curiouser and curiouser." Here Paul faced a literal "open door" but chose not to walk through it. What would you have done? Why?

10. Read verses 29–34, looking for all the specific results of Paul's "curious" action. Tell of a time when the "kingdom results" of your following what you sensed to be God's will became obvious to you only after the fact of your obedience.

11. Finish the story, reading verses 35–40. Wouldn't it have been easier for Paul to slip out of town and "not make waves"? Discuss a situation in your past where it seemed best not to slink away in silence but to take a stand.

12. Take one more look at Acts 16:40, the last reported action that Paul took before leaving town. As you continue your journey in and with God's will, what precautions can you take to ensure that you will not forget to encourage others in their walk?

13. Consider this whole firsthand account of Paul's visit to Philippi. Did Paul ever seem fretful about whether or not he was making the right move? Give a one-sentence summary of the one thing you want to remember from this "Paul visits Philippi" passage.

When action is needed, light will come.
J. I. PACKER

IT'S NOT MAGIC ❧ 58

Friendship Boosters

Luke's "Paul in Philippi" account begins and ends with Lydia welcoming fellow believers into her home—an act of hospitality. "Count off" by twos and with a partner, agree to meet for a brief cup of coffee later in the week. If meeting in one of your homes just won't work, agree to meet at a public place—maybe at "the river" or a park, another gathering place for Lydia and friends. If you want a set agenda, try this: Both of you plan to bring and talk about a picture (painting or photo) or a reading (poem or paragraph) through which you have learned something about God and his ways.

Just for Fun

Consider the following quote by Philip Yancey:

God does not paint by numbers.

Yancey's words might be easier to remember if you have a little fun with a set of children's watercolors (or crayons) and a piece of blank paper. Paint or draw a free-form picture of your day so far. Include some element that represents the presence of God. Explain your picture to the group.

Praying Together

Pray for each person individually, for faith, grace, and power (strength) to take the next step in her life journey. As you end your prayer together, focus on praise and thanksgiving—for God's grace in your lives, as he has led you each in unique ways that have brought you to this point where you are meeting with this group of encouraging women.

> *What the Lord is asking me, he is asking*
> *no one else....The call, this request is completely*
> *beyond my grasp, quite impossible—without his help.*
> *Yet even as he asks it, he makes it clear that he*
> *will give me the power to do what is needed.*
> *He will not leave me abandoned or alone. He does*
> *not ask the impossible. Our God does not play tricks.*
> EMILIE GRIFFIN

Making It Real
in Your Own Life

1. Turn again to the area of life in which you're looking for discernment. If the timing is right, take the next step— walking through an open door. Of course the timing may not be right. (God does not work in six-week study cycles, believe it or not!) Whether you are waiting or walking, live this week in faith, not in fear.

2. Every day this week, try to be consciously aware of one or more everyday, rather mundane, decision points. What decision are you making, and what is influencing your decision? Make some notes to increase your consciousness. Be careful not take on this "awareness" with fretfulness, but with awe and wonder at the variety of ways God uses to direct your walk as you trust him with your journey.

What If I've Misread the Signs?

At any season of life we may be distressed as we look back at the past because we think we've missed God's will. *I stepped left when I should have stepped right*, we lament. *How can I get back on track?*

Such regrets may surface for any number of reasons. Maybe, if we're honest, we'll admit we chose to ignore God's leading.

Or these "second thoughts" may come because our road has gotten bumpy. *How can a dip in the road be in God's will?* we wonder. *Wasn't the honeymoon supposed to last forever?* Sometimes in our search for "milk and honey" in the Promised Land, we forget that Jesus said, "In this world you will have trouble" (John 16:33).

These are the issues we'll look at in this last session: *What are we supposed to do if we think we've messed up, if we think we've misread the signs and missed God's good will?*

A Moment
for Quiet Reflection

1. Think of a time when it *seems* you made a wrong turn despite your attempts to hear and desire to follow God's will. Try to identify any negative feelings that surface when you think about that part of your life journey. (Angry? Guilty? Regretful? Remorseful? Shamed? . . .)

2. Spend an equal amount of time and effort trying to identify any positive feelings that surface when you think about that event or season of life. If positive "feelings" come hard, think in terms of positive outcomes or lessons learned.

3. When you go to the Bible study session, take with you a bottle or two of your favorite perfumes.

> *Only later, after the trauma [of seeming failure] was over, was I able to . . .distinguish between missing God's mark and the trembling of a wounded psyche. I smile a lot more because now I know the difference between being sinful and being human. We are acting sinfully when we disobey a principle outlined in God's written revelation. We are acting humanly when we act according to the limitations imposed on homo sapiens.*
> MARION DUCKWORTH

Knowing God's Heart

1. Sometimes our "missing God's mark" may be the result of our own willful disobedience. Read Psalm 32:3–11. In what sorry state does the psalmist start out? If you were feeling this way and wanted to write a psalm, how would you word it?

2. What pattern does the psalmist provide us for moving "beyond the negative"?

3. Tell of a time when you have been like a willful animal that had to be reined in—rather than having trust in God's leadership in your life.

4. Tell of a time when the Lord's unfailing love surrounded you as you trusted in him.

5. Read 2 Corinthians 2:12–16; 3:5. Perceiving that *God* had "opened a door," Paul went to Troas. But once there, Paul "had no peace of mind." Does Paul seem concerned that he has made a mistake—or walked through the wrong door? What does his reaction say to you as you think about your perceived "mistakes" in doing God's will?

6. Let's say that you, in faith, have walked through an "open door." But then you have "no peace." How might you determine whether you should "say good-bye" or stay on course? (To answer this question, draw on what you've learned in this whole study.)

7. Consider the wonderful image of Christ leading you as in a procession and your very life being a walking atomizer, spreading the perfume of Christ. If you are walking in faith—one step at a time—how can you "spread the aroma" even if you *feel* as if you've taken a wrong turn? Brainstorm and share ideas.

8. Read Hebrews 3:12–15, looking for "do" and "do not" instructions for believers. Reorganize the instruction in terms of three time frames.

   • Past

   • Present

   • Future

9. Read Jude, verses 18–23. Using the three categories given below, name the direct and indirect instructions given here to believers wanting to do God's will.

- My relationship with God

- My relationship with other Christians

- My relationship with non-Christians

10. Read Jude 24–25. What promises do these verses offer you as you close this study and look to the future?

> *Now we see but a poor reflection as in a mirror;*
> *then we shall see face to face. Now I know in part;*
> *then I shall know fully, even as I am fully known.*
> 1 CORINTHIANS 13:12

Friendship Boosters

1. Turn again to the prayers taped inside the front and back covers of this book. Work together to clarify any niggling questions. If questions remain, what insights from the Scriptures in this last lesson can help you encourage one another to keep seeking God and his direction?

2. Pretend you're teenagers visiting a department store perfume counter. If women remembered to bring along perfume samples, introduce your friends to your old or new favorite scents. Remind each other that you are the "aroma of Christ."

Just for Fun

To help you remember that God "leads us in triumphal procession in Christ," play (or sing) some lively music, maybe contemporary praise music. Then "fall into" a line, putting your hands on the shoulders or waist of the person in front of you. Dance a joyful "snake dance." Rotate leaders often to remind yourselves that God, not a human, is the procession's leader.

Praying Together

Pray together for each woman individually, as she continues her daily walk in faith. Say (or sing) this verse of a prayer-hymn, "O Jesus, I Have Promised," by John Ernest Bode.

> O let me hear You speaking
> In accents clear and still,
> Above the storms of passion,
> The murmurs of self-will;
> O speak to reassure me,
> To hasten or control;
> O speak, and make me listen,
> Thou Guardian of my soul.

Then end your prayer with the closing "doxology" of Jude (verses 24–25): "To him who is able to keep you from falling and to present you before his glorious presence without fault and with great joy—to the only God our Savior be glory, majesty, power and authority, through Jesus Christ our Lord, before all ages, now and forevermore! Amen."

> *Following God is not like walking a tightrope.*
> ELEANOR VANDEVORT

Making It Real in Your Own Life

1. In prayer (and maybe with a journal) present your past "wrong turns"—real or perceived—to God, with confession, with a prayer for mercy, with gratitude for his love and grace that works in and through you (and sometimes despite you).

2. Write a one-sentence statement that identifies one principle you want to remember from this study—one principle you want to "guard" in your heart.

> *The Counselor, the Holy Spirit, whom the Father will send in my name, will teach you all things and will remind you of everything I have said to you. Peace I leave with you; my peace I give you. I do not give to you as the world gives. Do not let your hearts be troubled and do not be afraid.*
>
> JOHN 14:26–27

LEADER'S GUIDE

LESSON ONE

1. An immediate answer to this question might be "obeying him." But you might push discussion by laying out this comment of one woman: "I'd obey God if he'd just make it clear what he wanted me to do." *(Why doesn't he send me an angelic message?)*

3. You might refer to Luke 12:48 as a discussion starter: "From everyone who has been given much, much will be demanded."

6. Note that there are virtually no details as to how her life will progress after the immediate conception of this holy child. The child will be a son, to be named Jesus. He will be called the Son of God. He will be king of the Jews. Mary was being asked to accept the "assignment" by faith.

10. Consider, for example, twelve years later, when Jesus was lost in Jerusalem. (See Luke 2:41–52.) Can you imagine her pleading for another visit from Gabriel? She would be repeatedly challenged to continue to "believe that what the Lord has said to her would be accomplished" (Luke 1:45). Compare Luke 8:19–21 with the parallel account in Matthew 12:46–50.

12. Note that Luke notes this reflective nature of Mary a second time, in Luke 2:51, so this must have been an obvious part of who she was.

   Just for Fun. You will need to provide paper and art supplies for this project.

LESSON TWO

2. Verse 15 may be confusing. *The NIV Study Bible* gives this explanation: "One who does not have the Spirit is not qualified to judge the spiritual person. Thus believers are not rightfully subject to the opinions of unbelievers."

3. Note that Romans 11:34 quotes again the Old Testament challenge Paul cited in 1 Corinthians 2:16: "Who has known the mind of the Lord?" Paul praises God's grandeur (Rom. 11:36) and then continues, with Romans 12:1: "Therefore . . . in view of God's mercy . . ."

4. If discussion starts slowly, you might point out the second item in the "Making It Real" section at the end of the lesson (reading Scripture, in this case Proverbs). Refer also to Philippians 4:8, a list of renewed thought patterns: whatever is true, noble, right, pure . . . What can you do to enhance these thought patterns?

5. Possible reasons: the desire to be "safe" from God's anger or displeasure; the wish to be able to walk by sight, not by faith.

10. The word *saint* means someone who is holy or sanctified.

LESSON THREE

6. Answer first in literal, physical terms. If possible, let a door into your meeting room be closed but not locked and maybe not even latched. You might use it as a physical "prop." Just a slight nudge of the elbow or hip might open it. Or maybe a turn of the knob. And then of course one must "walk through." Then turn to the spiritual metaphor of "open doors." Might a "closed" door sometimes just need a nudge or a turn of the handle? Paul (verse 13) seems to indicate that he had tried to go to Rome but had been "prevented." Matthew 7:7 says, "Ask and it will be given to you; seek and you will find; knock and the door will be opened." Lead from this question right into question 7.

9. Consider this quote by Elisabeth Elliot *(God's Guidance):* "Sometimes ... we are in a quandary because we have already been shown what we ought to do and we are not satisfied with it. We are saying, 'Lord, when are you going to tell me?' and the truth is that he has told us."

LESSON FOUR

2. God does not want us to be paralyzed by fear; he does not give us a "spirit of fear" (see 2 Timothy 1:7 KJV). His peace can and does rule in our hearts. But as Sheila Walsh says, "I think we misunderstand what courage is. It's not the absence of fear; it's the presence of God in the midst of fear." As the title of a recent self-help book says, sometimes we should *Feel the Fear and Do It Anyway.* Sometimes peace comes as we face what we are afraid of.

4. To save time looking up verses, at the beginning of this question-discussion, assign each woman to look up one verse to read aloud. Go around the room, reading all six verses, quickly naming any principle for discerning an appropriate action: (a) guided by integrity; (b) guided by advice; (c) guided by love and self-discipline (a sound mind), not fear or timidity; (d) guided by "open doors" (focus on the "because open door ..." and note that opposition is not necessarily a "closed door"); (e) guided by acting "to the glory of God"; (f) guided by Scriptures. Then ask women to discuss an impending decision. How do these guidelines influence their decisions? Not everyone will be able to discuss every verse as it relates to an upcoming intended action.

5. To answer this question, you might suggest rephrasing verses 16–17 in their own (contemporary) words. What does it mean to "flee on horses," for instance?

Phillips Brooks (who wrote "O Little Town of Bethlehem") once said, "I believe I have spent half my life waiting for God to catch up with me." Know the feeling? Wanting to "run with" every "impression" or "call"?

9. Confirmation that something was "right" sometimes seems to come as we act—and almost as if a light showing the way were shining down over our shoulder.

10. Note verse 22. Following God will mean throwing some "idols" out of our lives. The menstrual cloth image is very powerful!

LESSON FIVE

3. In interpreting this dream, Paul obviously concluded it to mean God wanted him to go to Macedonia. It seems the traveling party agreed together to go—rather than Paul making an authoritative "decree" without agreement among his companions. This may give us some anecdotal guide for decisions that affect more than ourselves. "God told me we should . . ." should not be used recklessly to intimidate others. God can and does make his way known to all who are listening.

4–5. It seems the group went to the river because experience or common sense told them that worshipers would be there. They stayed at Lydia's because Lydia "persuaded" them. Yes, we earlier saw that God's word to our spirit is "more than intuition." And yet our decisions—made within God's will—may be based on very "nonspiritual" common sense, intuition, and the persuasion of others.

6. Reasons might include very spiritual issues: Matthew 8:29 tells of demon-possessed men recognizing Jesus as the Son of God. (See also James 2:19: "Even the demons believe [in God]—and shudder.") Paul also may have been very "humanly" irritated at the disorder and disruption and/or "troubled" that this girl was being abused by her "owners."

7. This passage is talking specifically about calling out demons, but a few general points might be made to our dealing with "troublesome negatives." Note that Paul acted after "several days." He may have been trying to assess the situation—not making an overly hasty judgment ("test") or decision.

8. Summarize the intervening events in verses 20–24: Casting out the fortune-telling spirit landed Paul and Silas in prison—after they were "severely flogged."

11. A *public* acquittal might have been important to Paul but also to Lydia and the new church Paul was leaving behind as he continued his evangelistic journey.

Just for Fun. You will need to provide a few art supplies: paper, crayons or colored pencils or paints. If there is painting, you should talk with the hostess and have available a table with plastic tablecloth.

End quote by Emilie Griffin. You might refer back to lesson 2 where you talked about whether or not God plays "holy hide-and-seek."

Preparation for Lesson 6. Request that women bring a bottle or two of a favorite perfume to the next session.

LESSON SIX

4. You might personalize the discussion of this question: How has acknowledging/facing/confessing your sin moved you from guilt and heaviness to rejoicing?

5. Introduce 2 Corinthians 2 with this comment: Sometimes we may be sure we've "misread the signs" through our own stubbornness or disobedience. Other times we may be utterly convinced that we walked ahead "in good faith" and yet perceive that we "didn't get it right." Let's look at a passage that gives help on this. (When Paul stepped out in faith and yet had no peace of mind, it seems he did not spend energy dwelling on "what did I do wrong?" He simply took the next step. Do we sometimes get stuck dwelling on the past, when we should just take the "next step"?)

8. The past: Do not repeat the mistakes of the past. The present: Focus on hearing God's word today and doing his will today. Encourage others. Do not harden your hearts. The future: Persevere in faith and with confidence.

Friendship Boosters. Testing perfumes. Be sensitive to allergies among the group. Before the session you might go to a perfume counter or cosmetic distributor and ask if it's possible for you to get tiny sample tubes of fragrance for the group.

ⓘ FAITH

Women of Faith Bible studies are based on the popular
Women of Faith conferences.

Women of Faith is partnering with Zondervan Publishing House,
Integrity Music, *Today's Christian Woman* magazine, and Campus Crusade
to offer conferences, publications, worship music, and inspirational gifts
that support and encourage today's Christian women.

Since their beginning in January of 1996, the Women of Faith conferences
have enjoyed an enthusiastic welcome by women across the country.

Call 1-888-49-FAITH for the many conference locations and dates available.

www.women-of-faith.com

**See the following page for additional information
about Women of Faith products.**

Look for these faith-building resources from Women of Faith:

Friends Through Thick & Thin by Gloria Gaither, Peggy Benson,
   Sue Buchanan, and Joy Mackenzie
      Hardcover 0-310-21726-1

We Brake for Joy! by Patsy Clairmont, Barbara Johnson, Marilyn Meberg,
   Luci Swindoll, Sheila Walsh, and Thelma Wells
      Hardcover 0-310-22042-4

Bring Back the Joy by Sheila Walsh
      Hardcover 0-310-22023-8
      Audio Pages 0-310-22222-2

The Joyful Journey by Patsy Clairmont, Barbara Johnson,
   Marilyn Meberg, and Luci Swindoll
      Softcover 0-310-22155-2
      Audio Pages 0-310-21454-8

Joy Breaks by Patsy Clairmont, Barbara Johnson,
   Marilyn Meberg, and Luci Swindoll
      Hardcover 0-310-21345-2

Women of Faith Journal
      Journal 0-310-97634-0

Promises of Joy for Women of Faith
      Gift Book 0-310-97389-9

Words of Wisdom for a Woman of Faith
      Gift Book 0-310-97390-2

Prayers for a Woman of Faith
      Gift Book 0-310-97336-8

We want to hear from you. Please send your comments about this book
to us in care of the address below. Thank you.

ZondervanPublishingHouse
Grand Rapids, Michigan 49530
http://www.zondervan.com